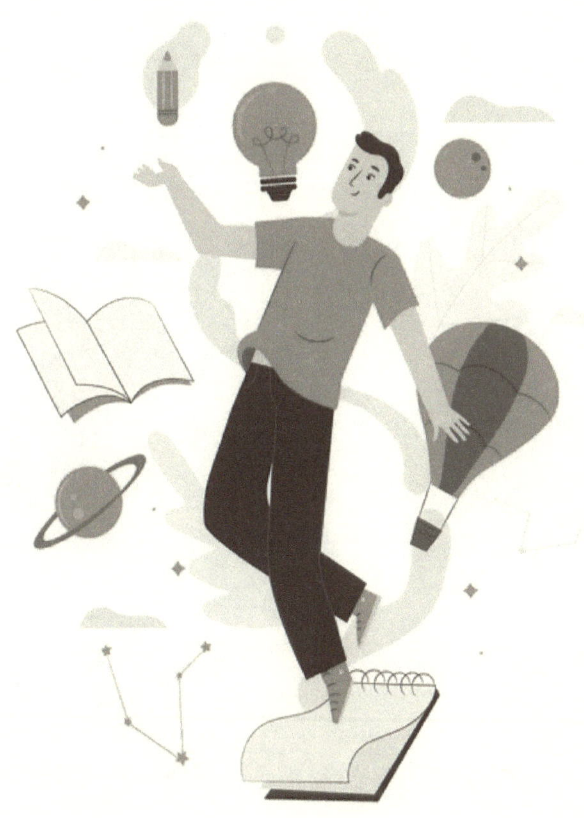

This coloring book belongs to:

____

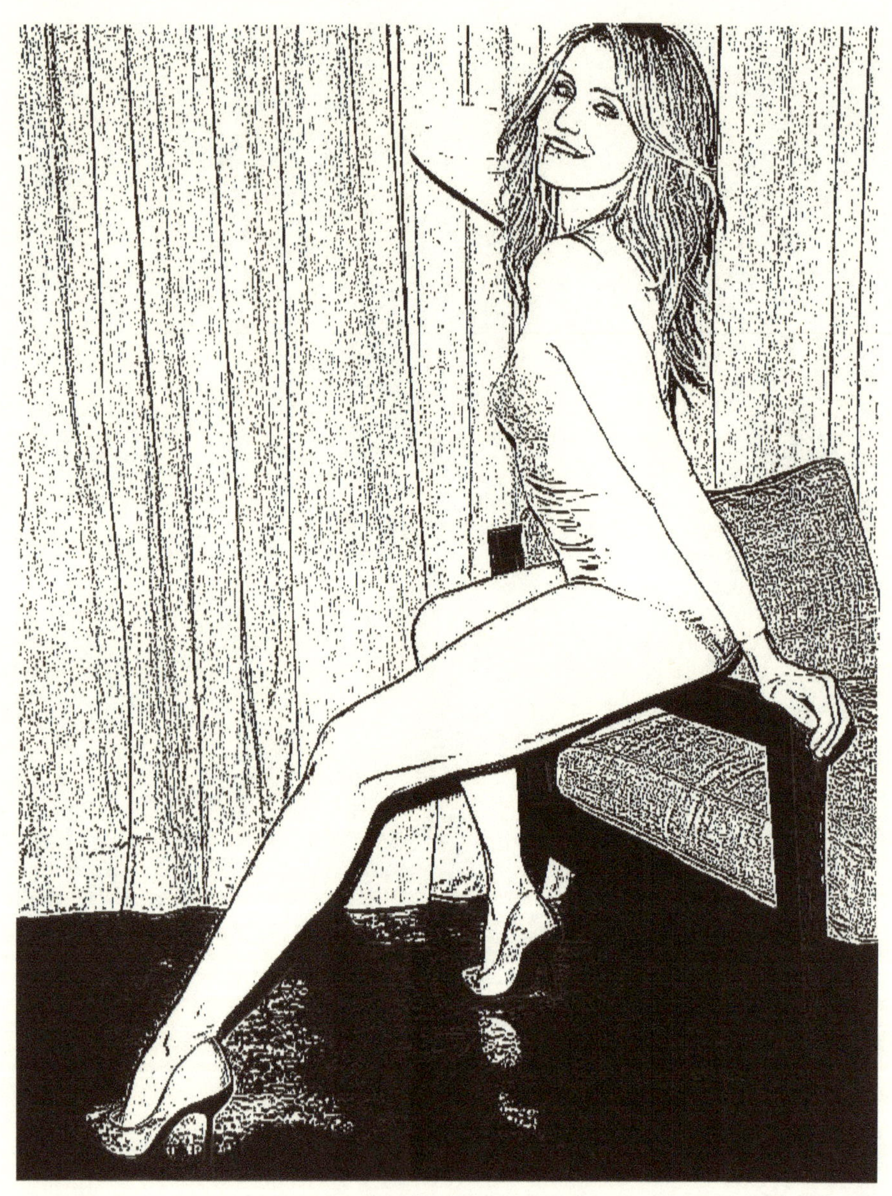

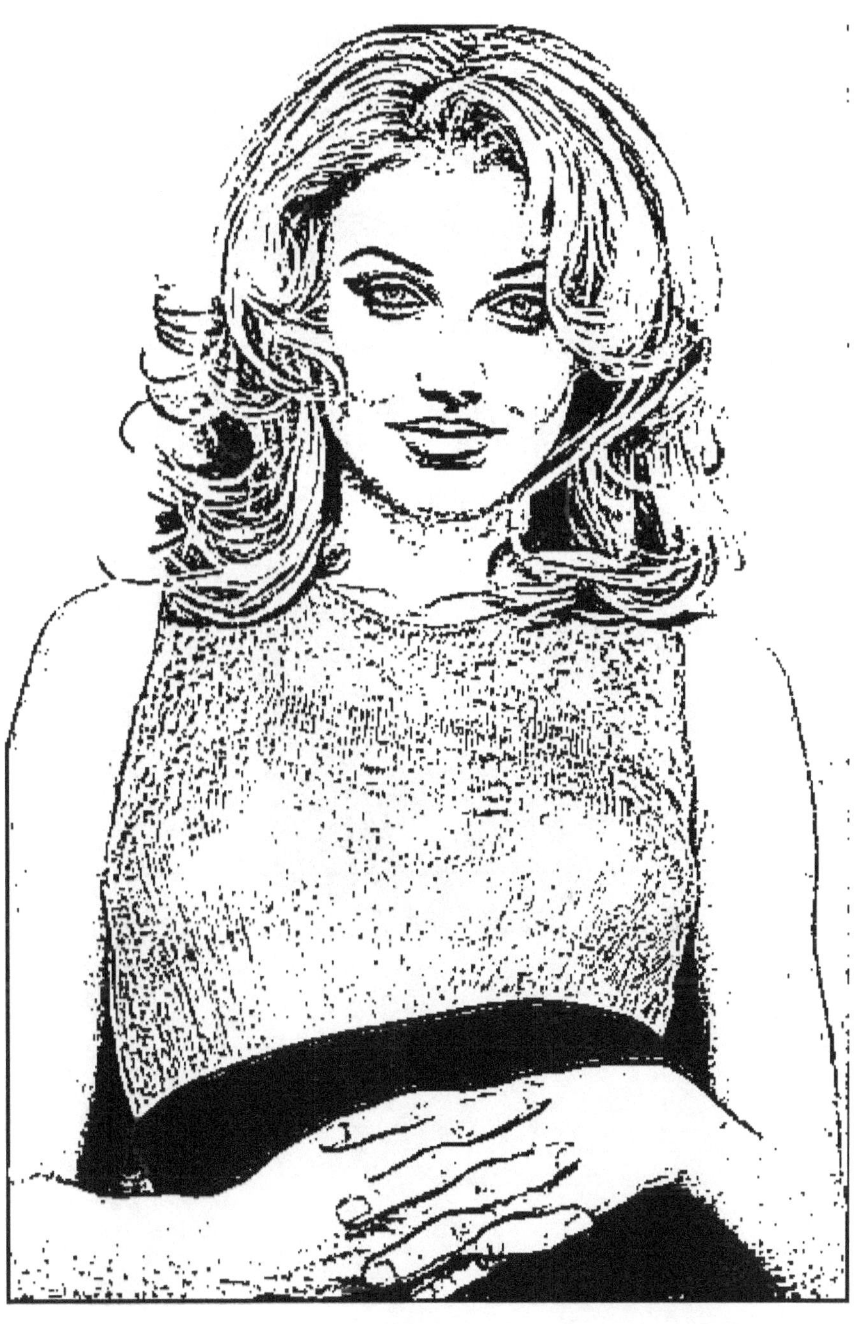

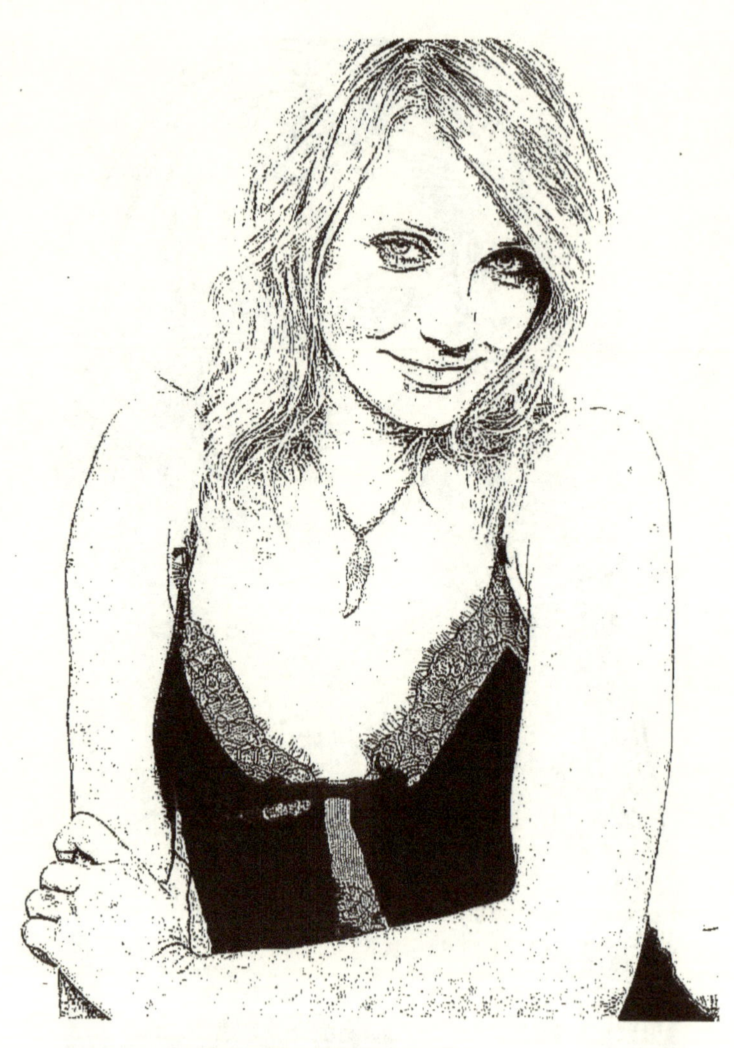

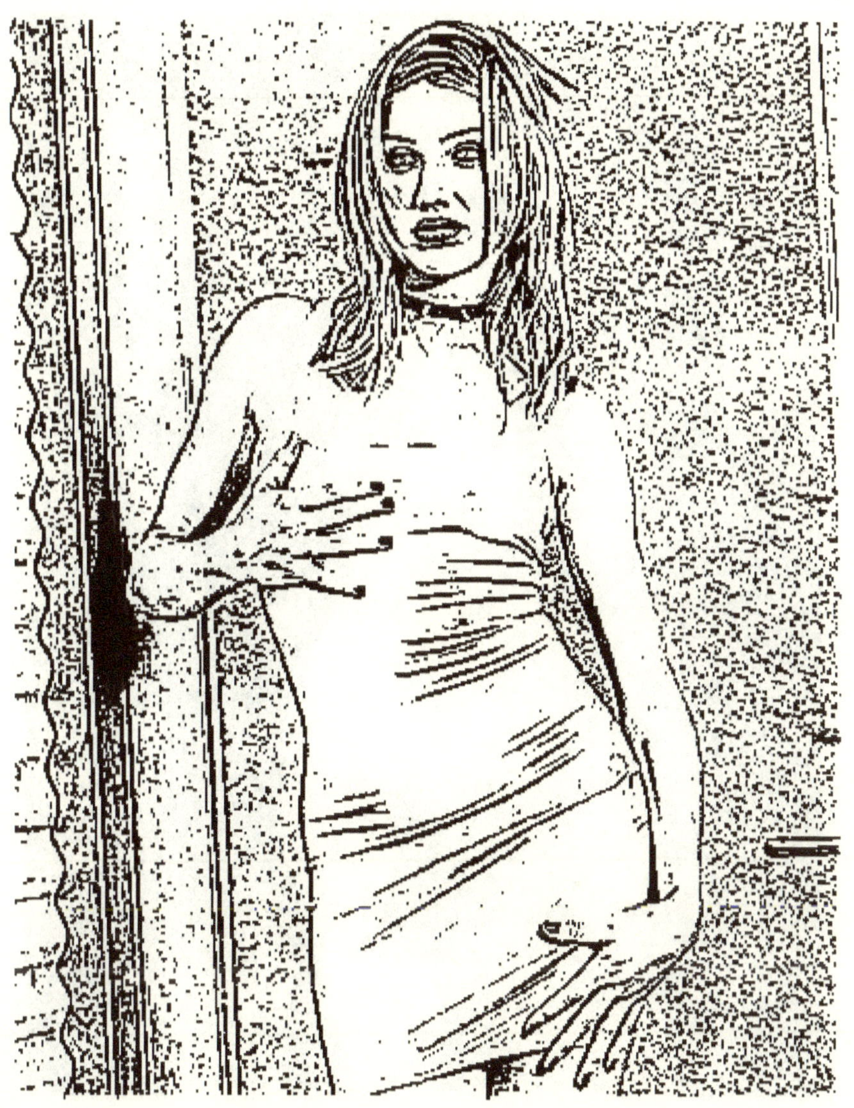

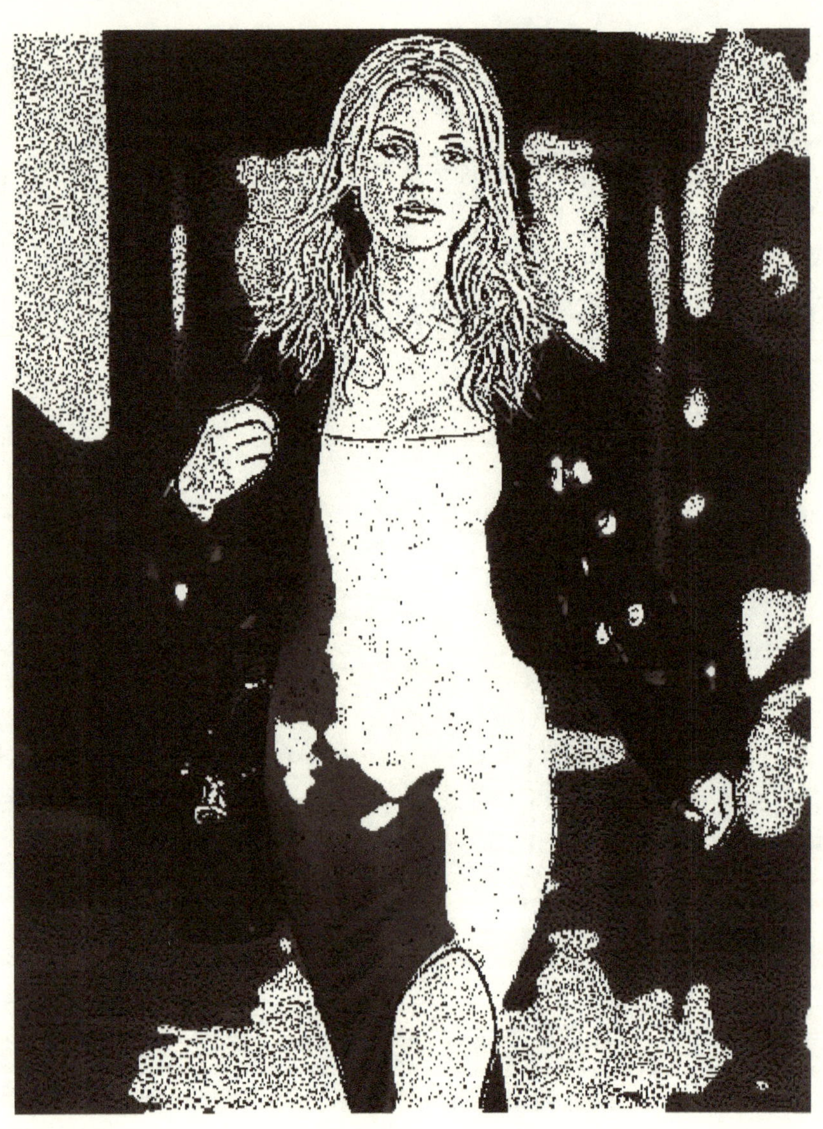

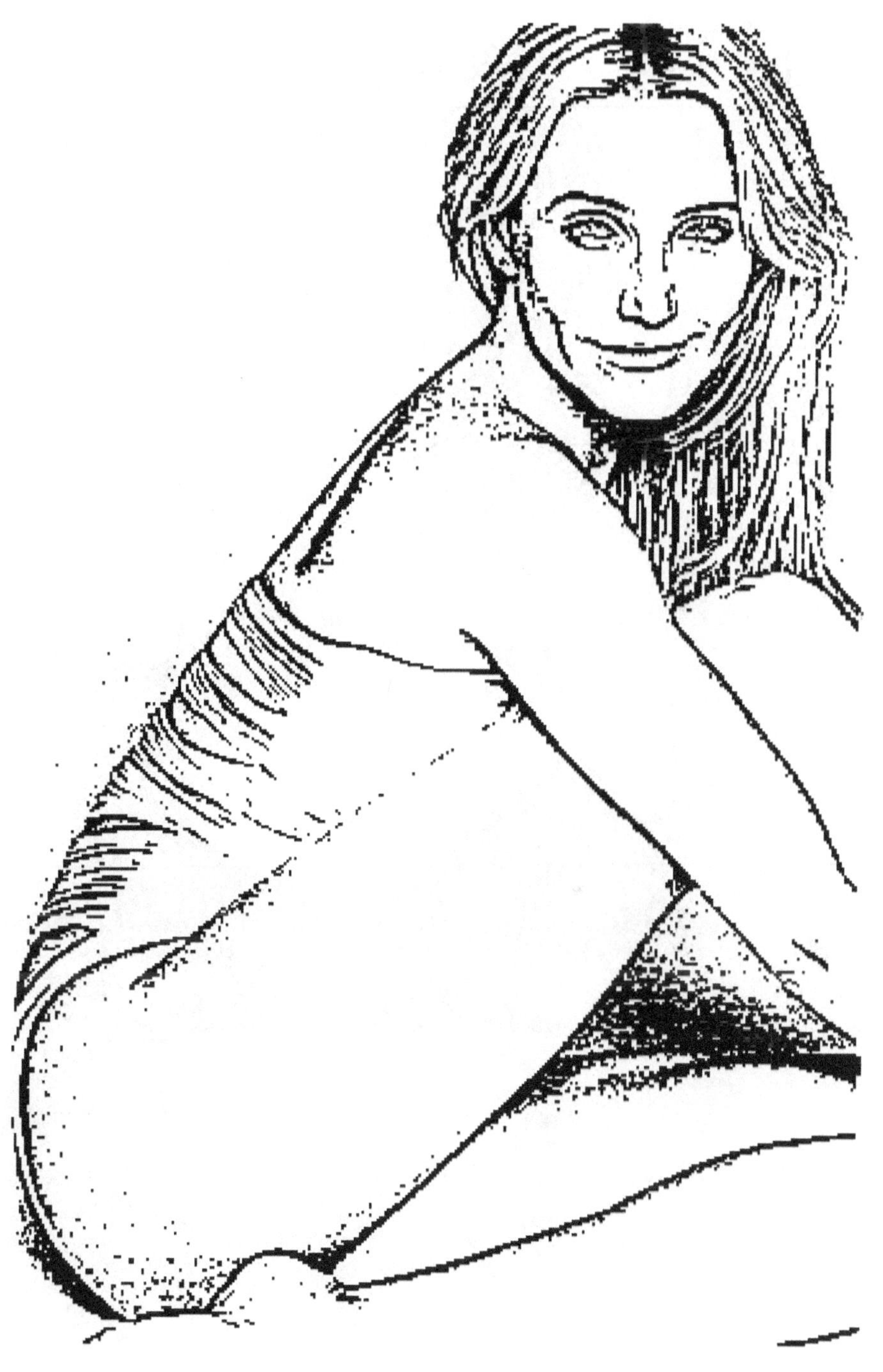

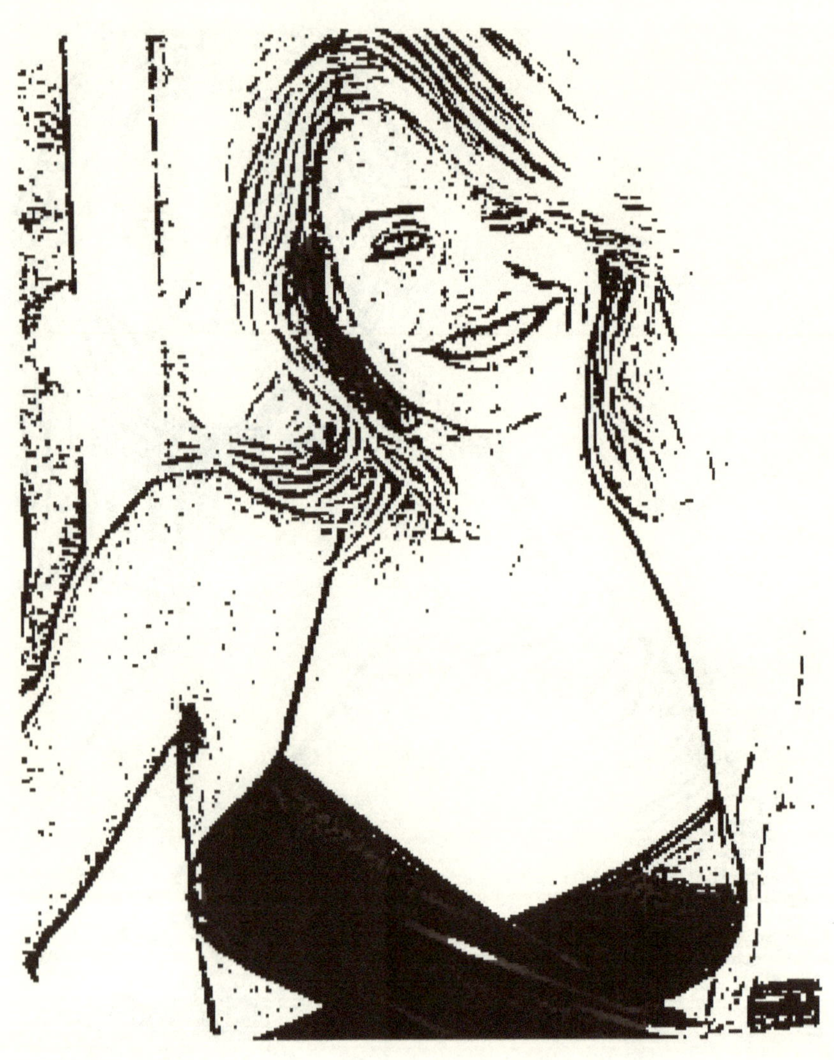

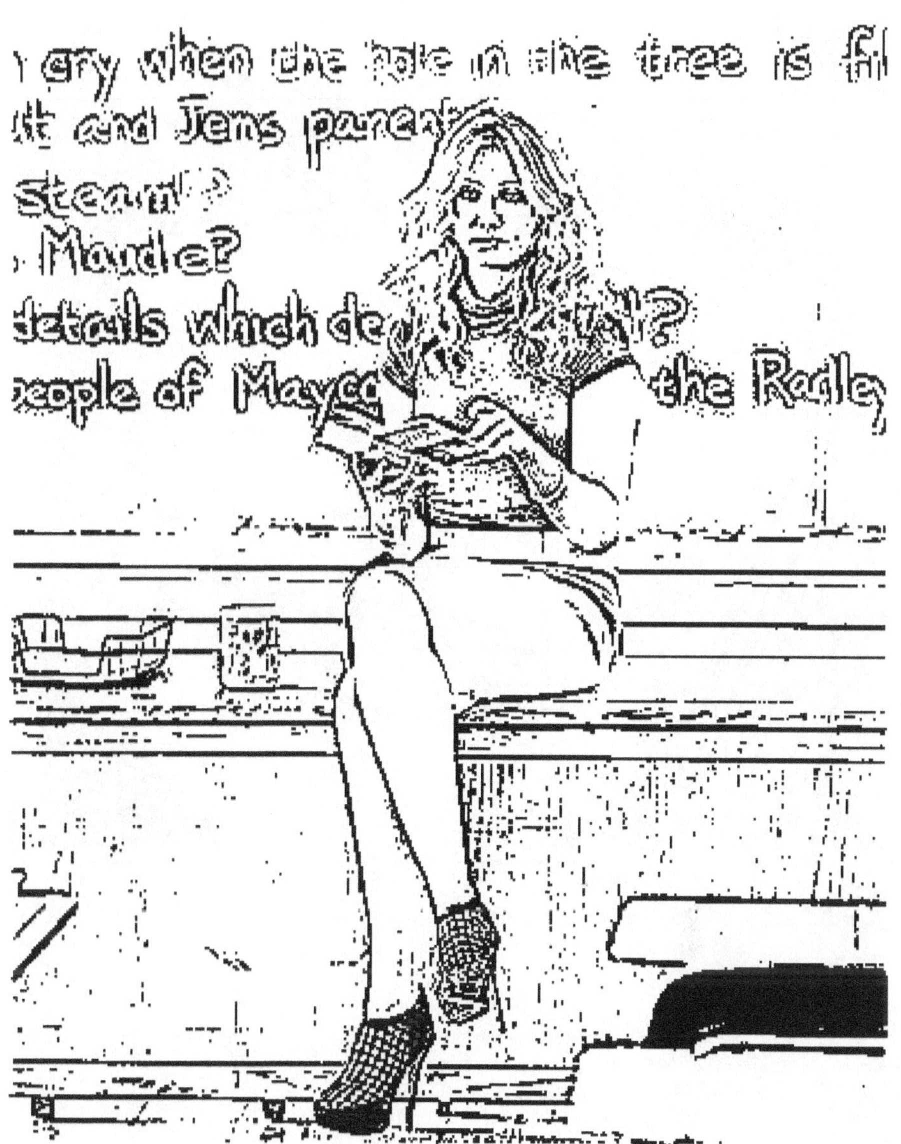

cry when the hole in the tree is fil
t and Jems parent
steam
Maudie?
details which de
people of Mayco   the Radle

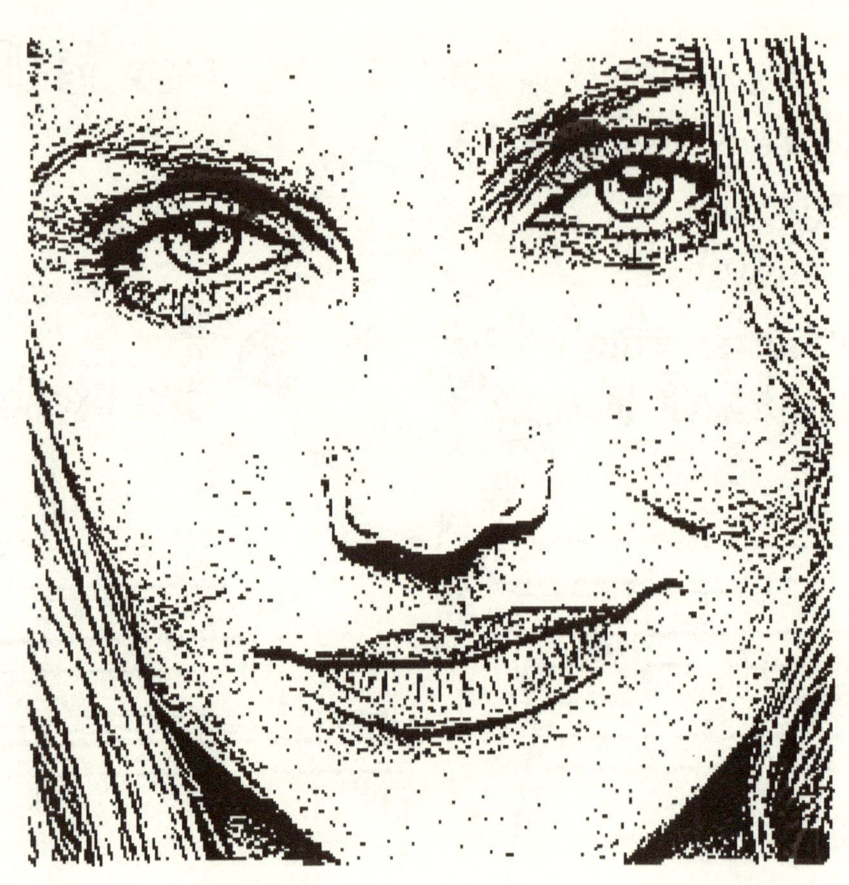

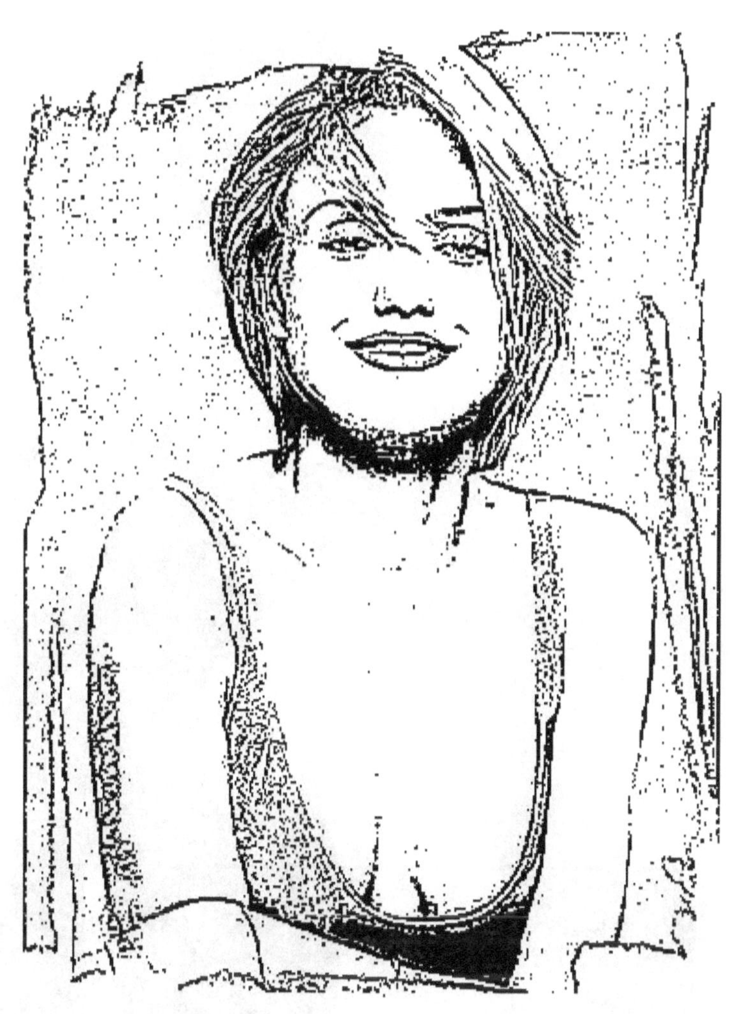

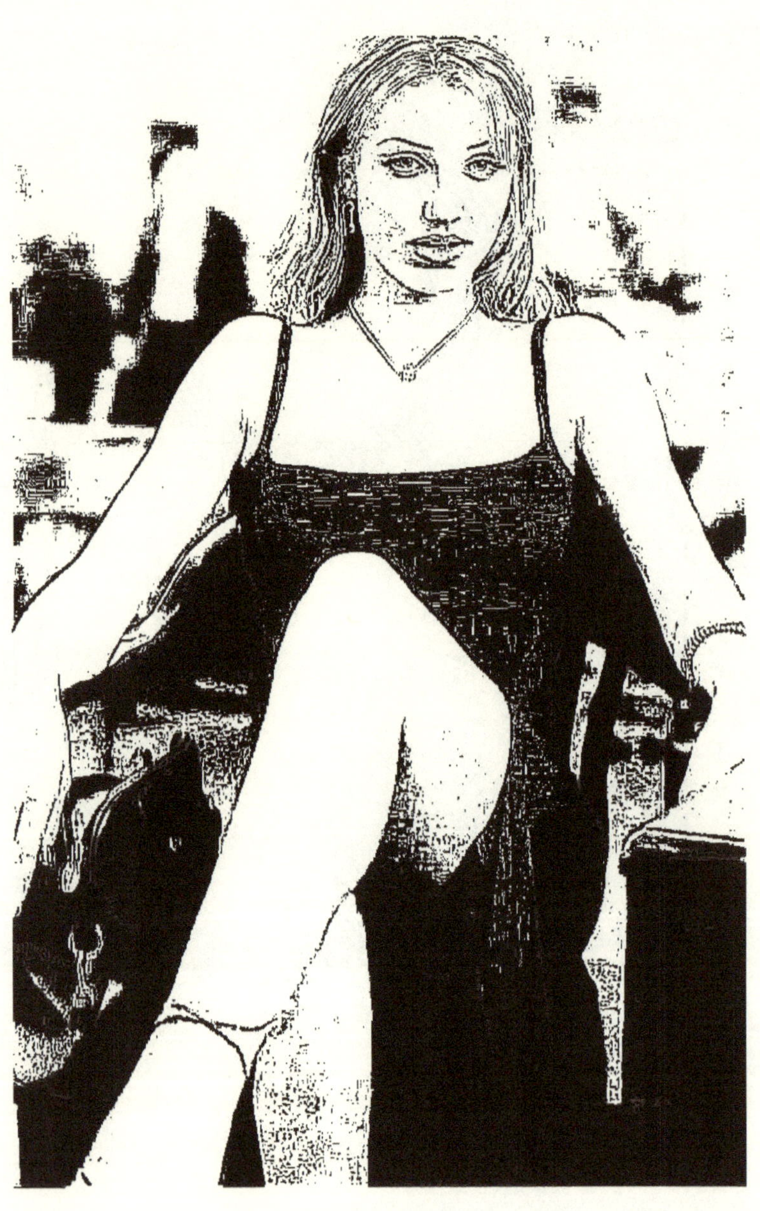

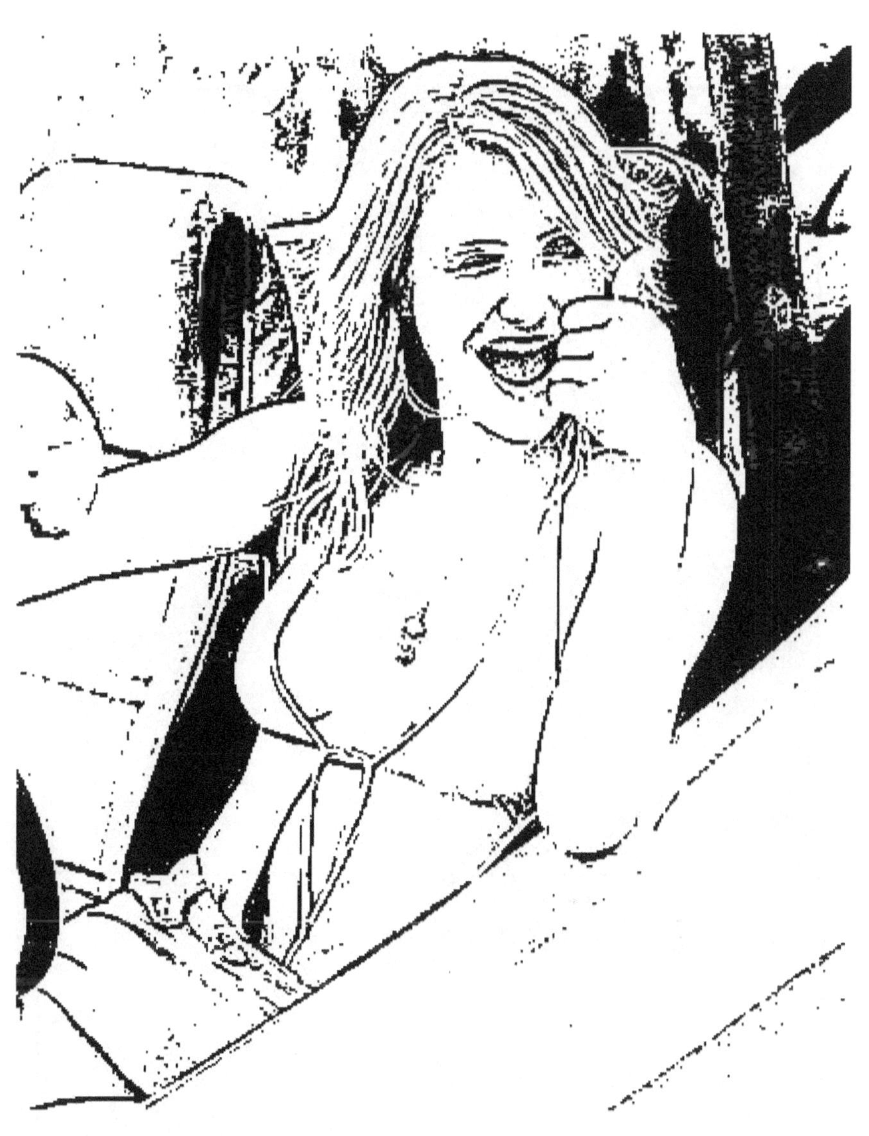

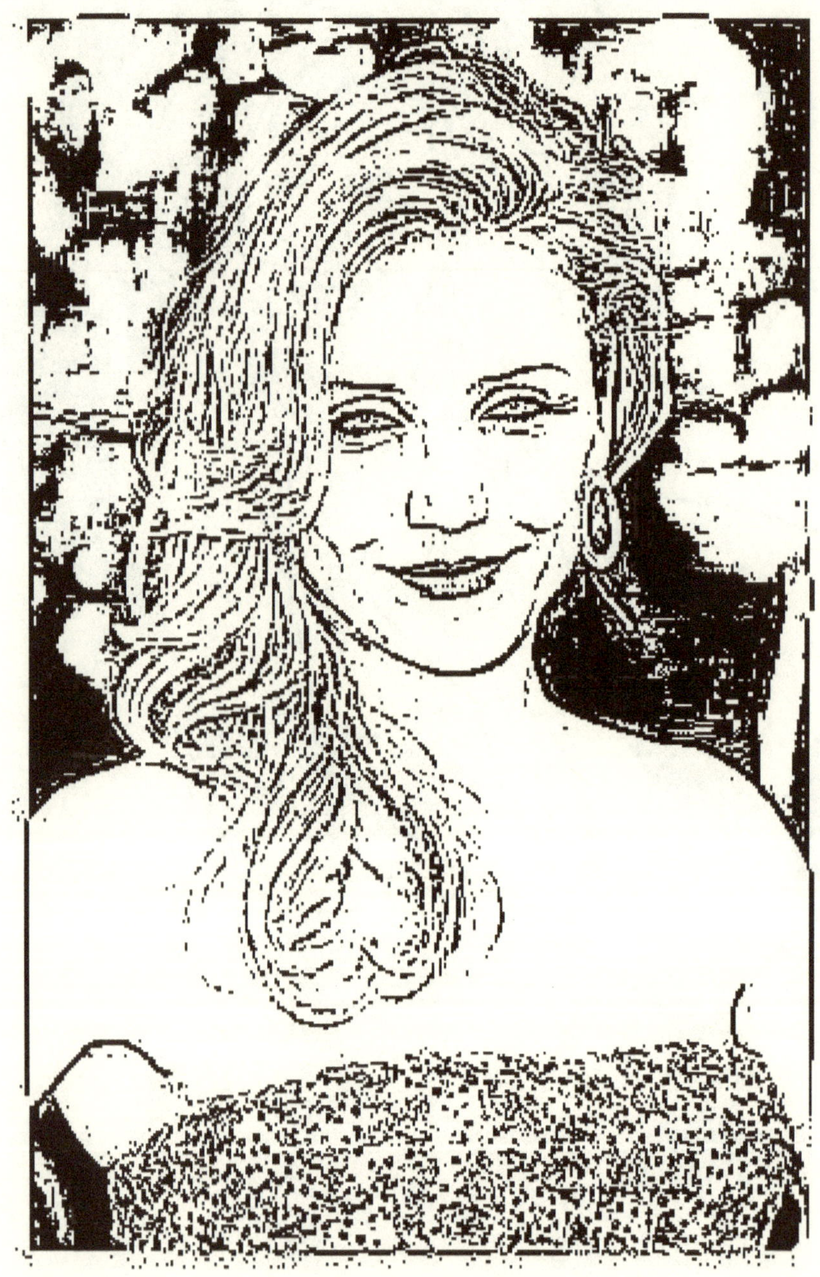

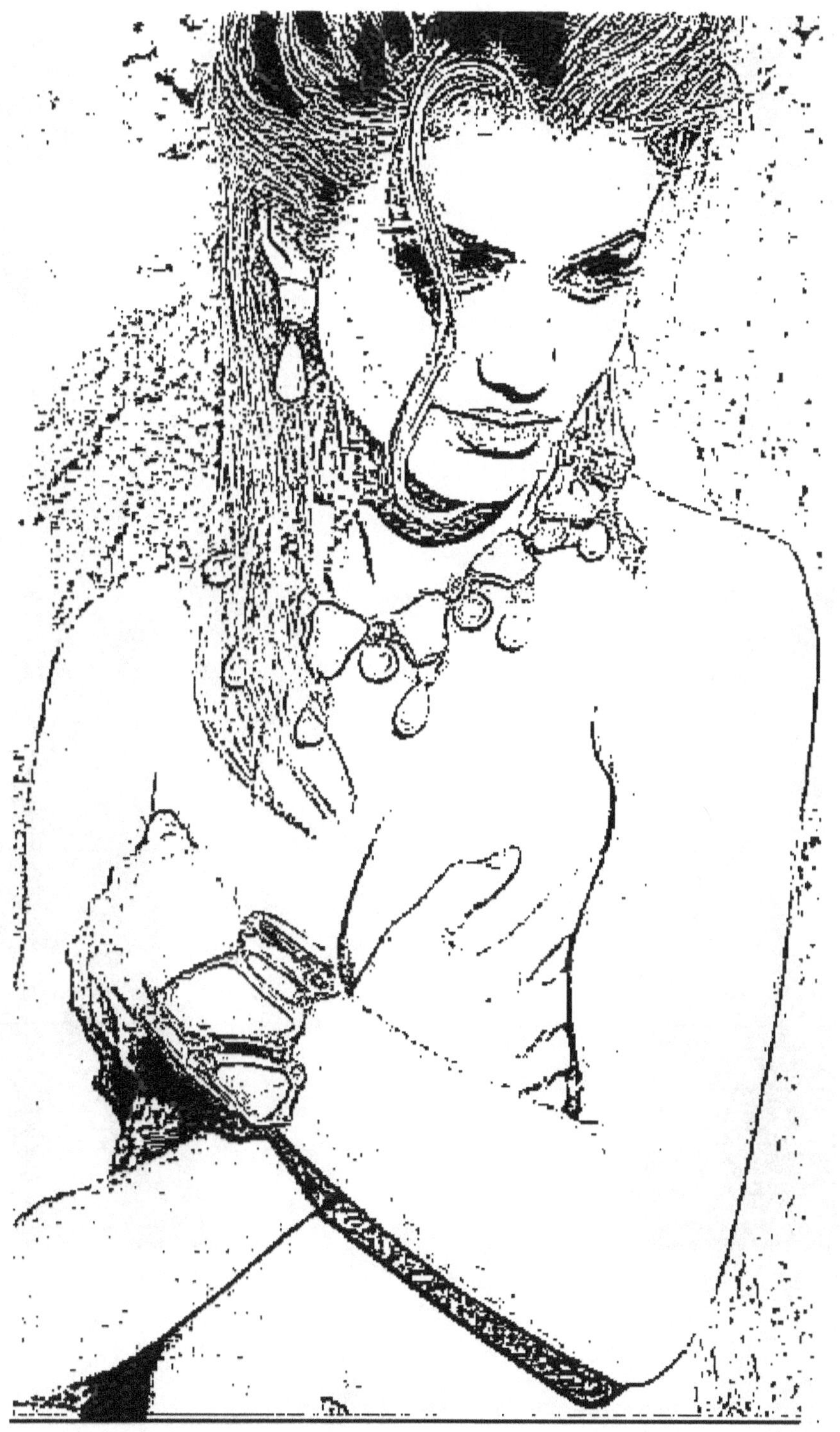

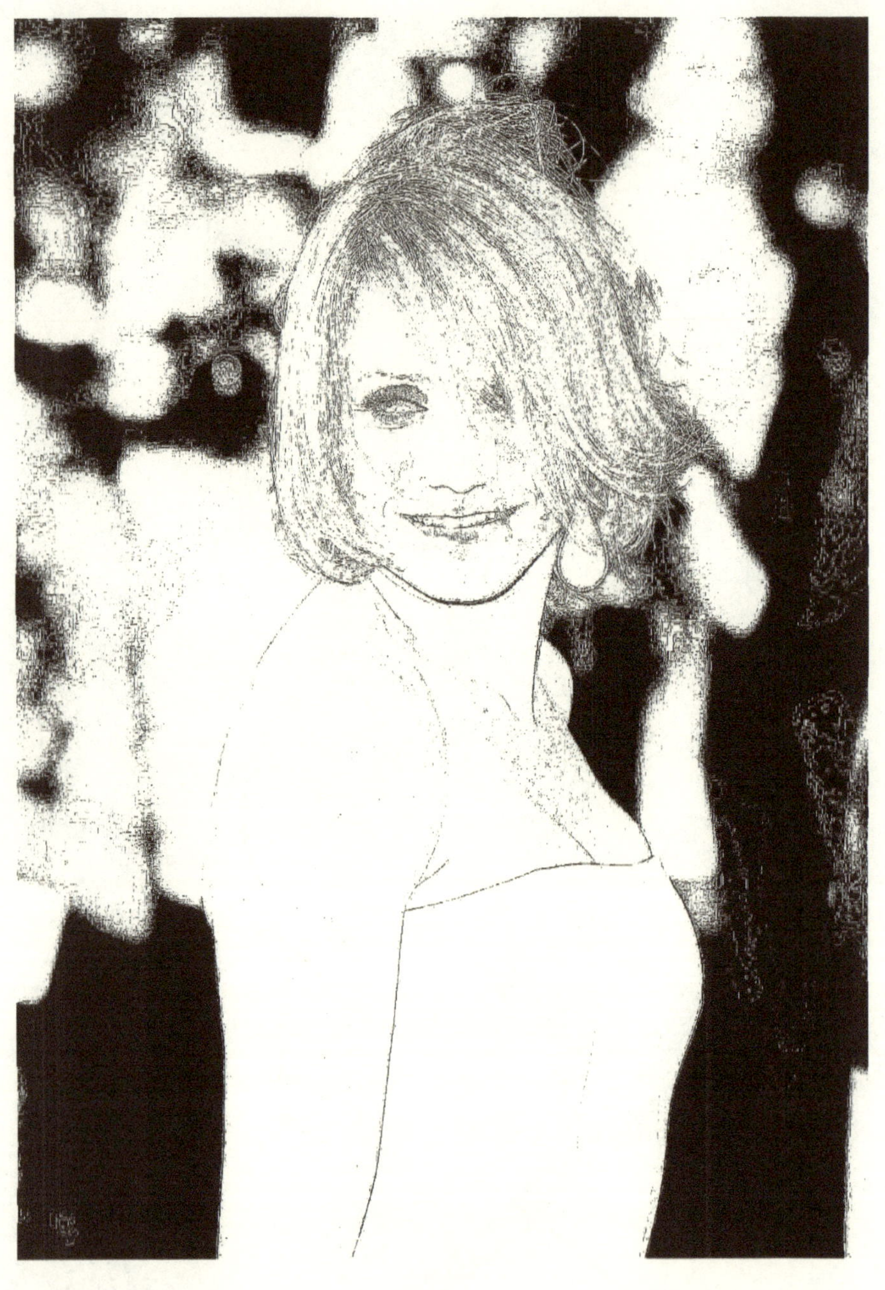

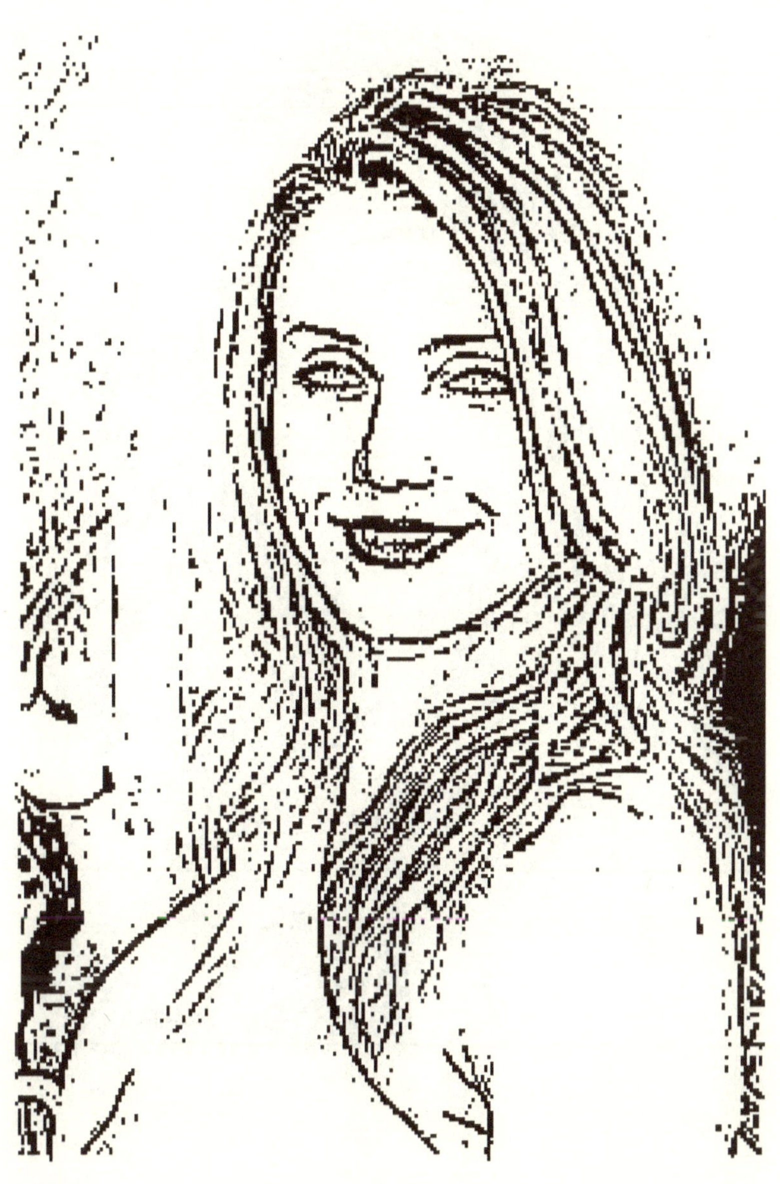

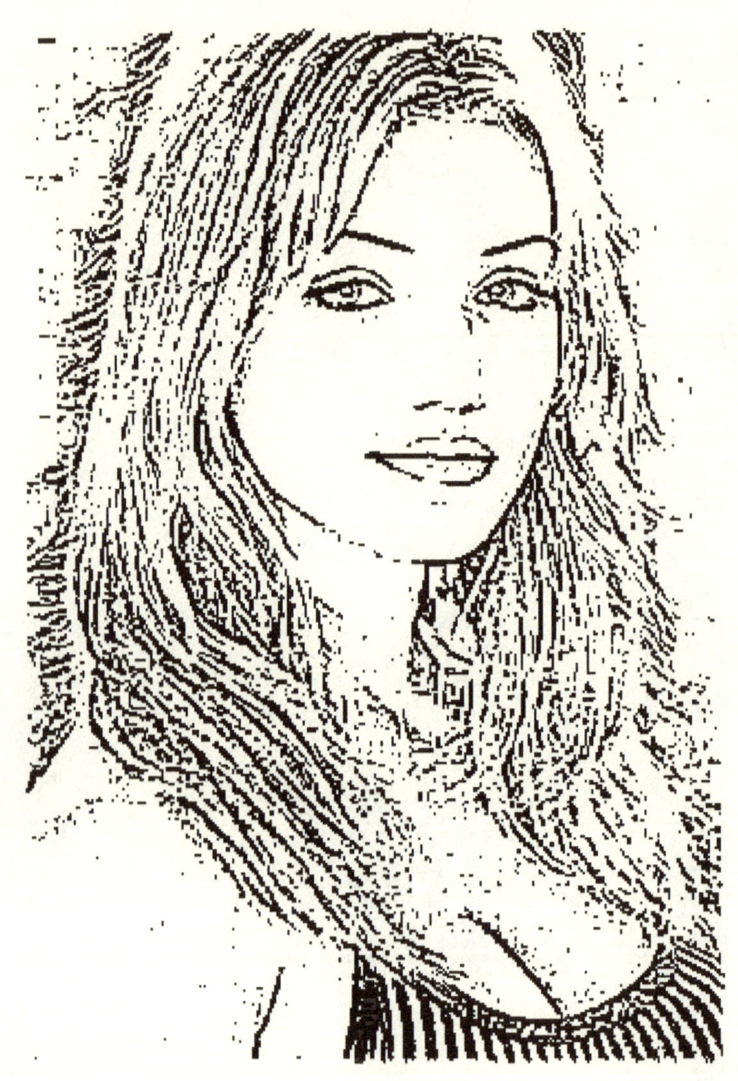

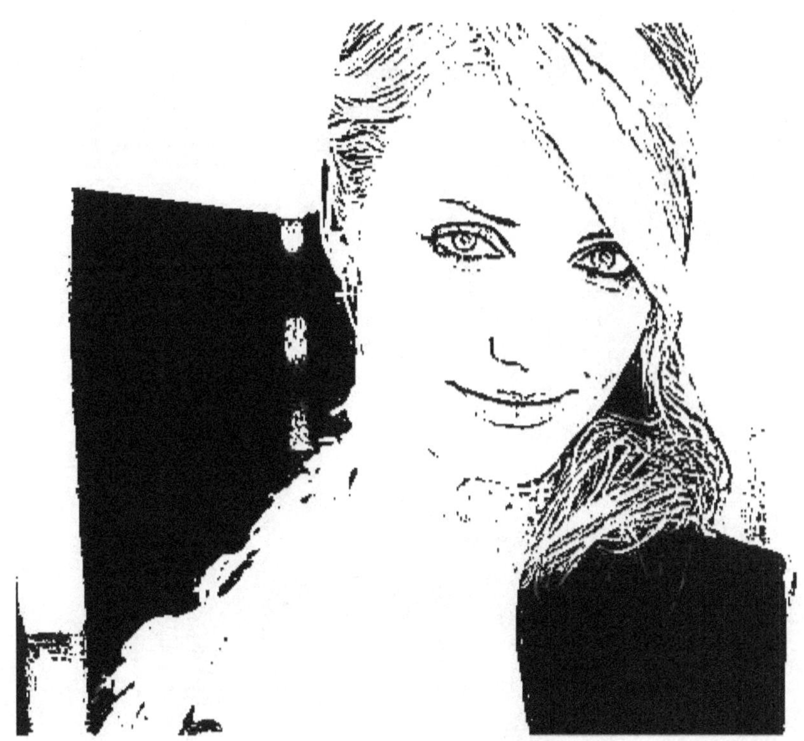

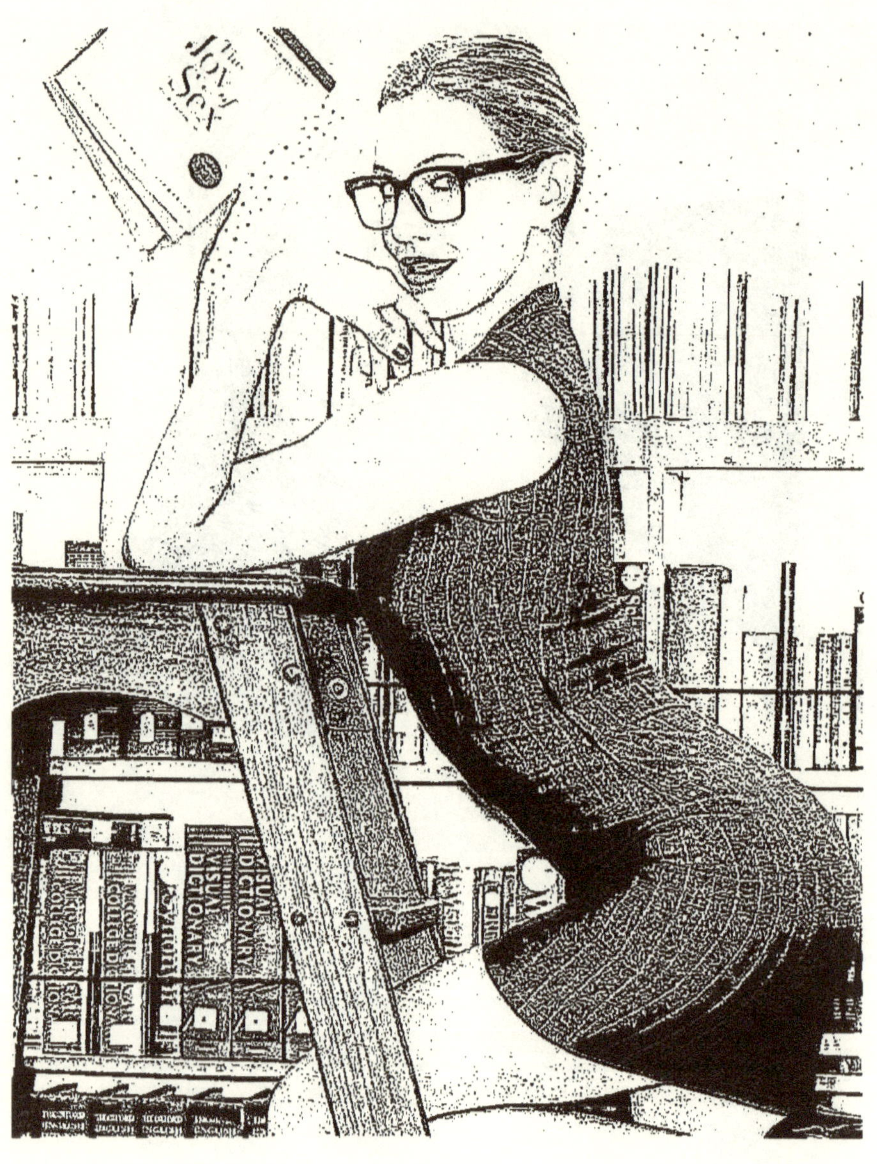

THE
JOY OF
SEX
VISUAL DICTIONARY
VISUAL DICTIONARY

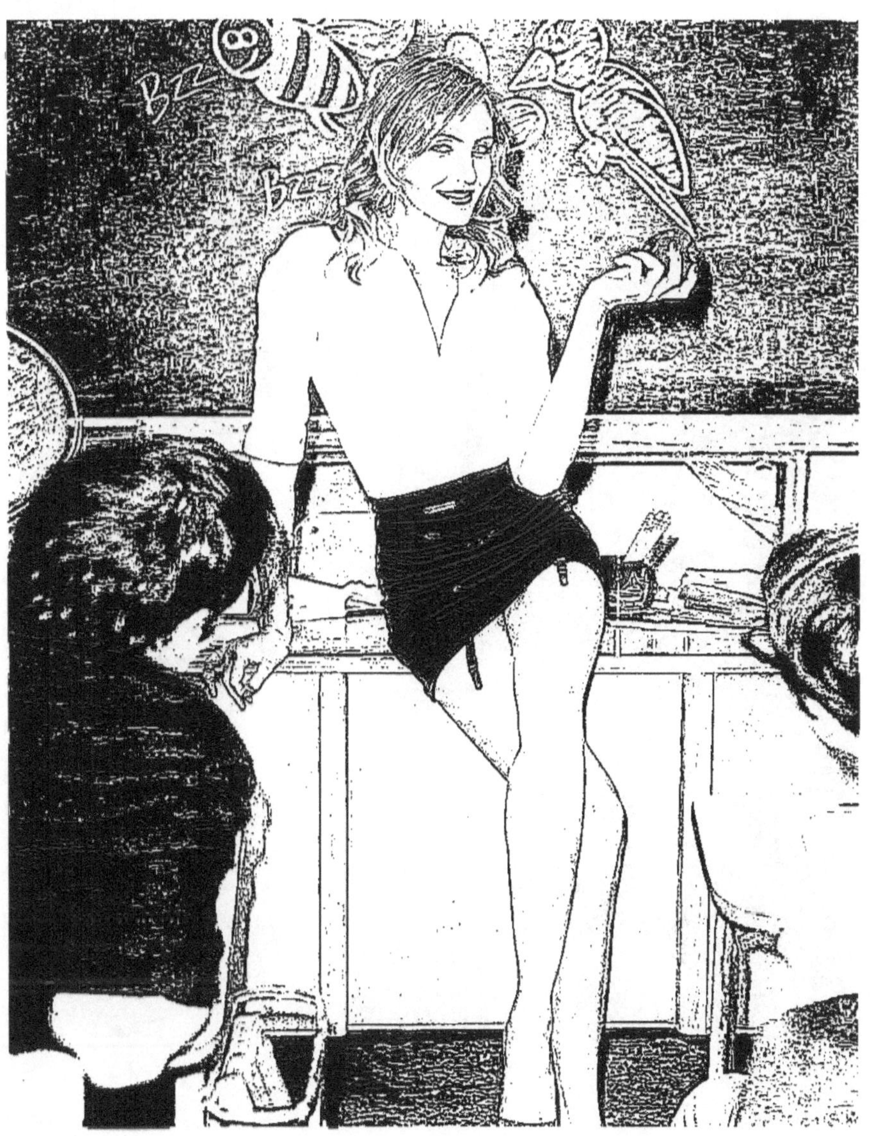
Bzz
Bzz

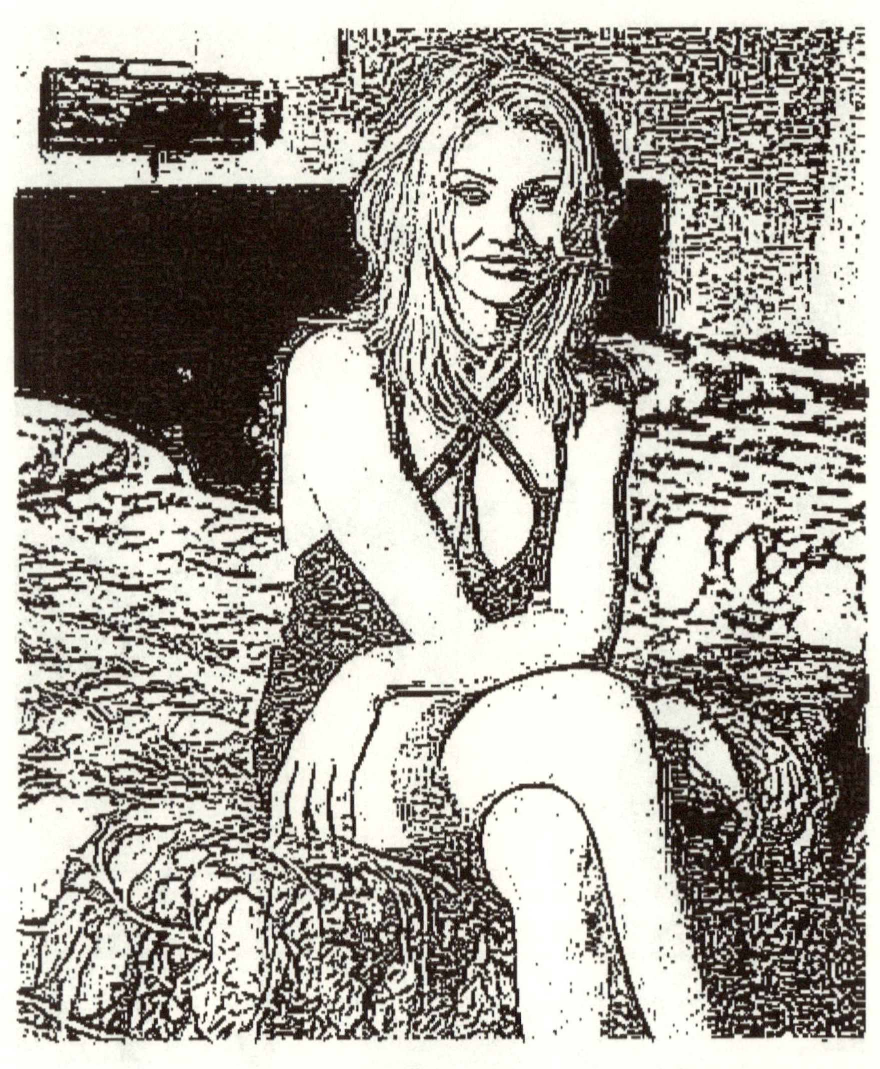

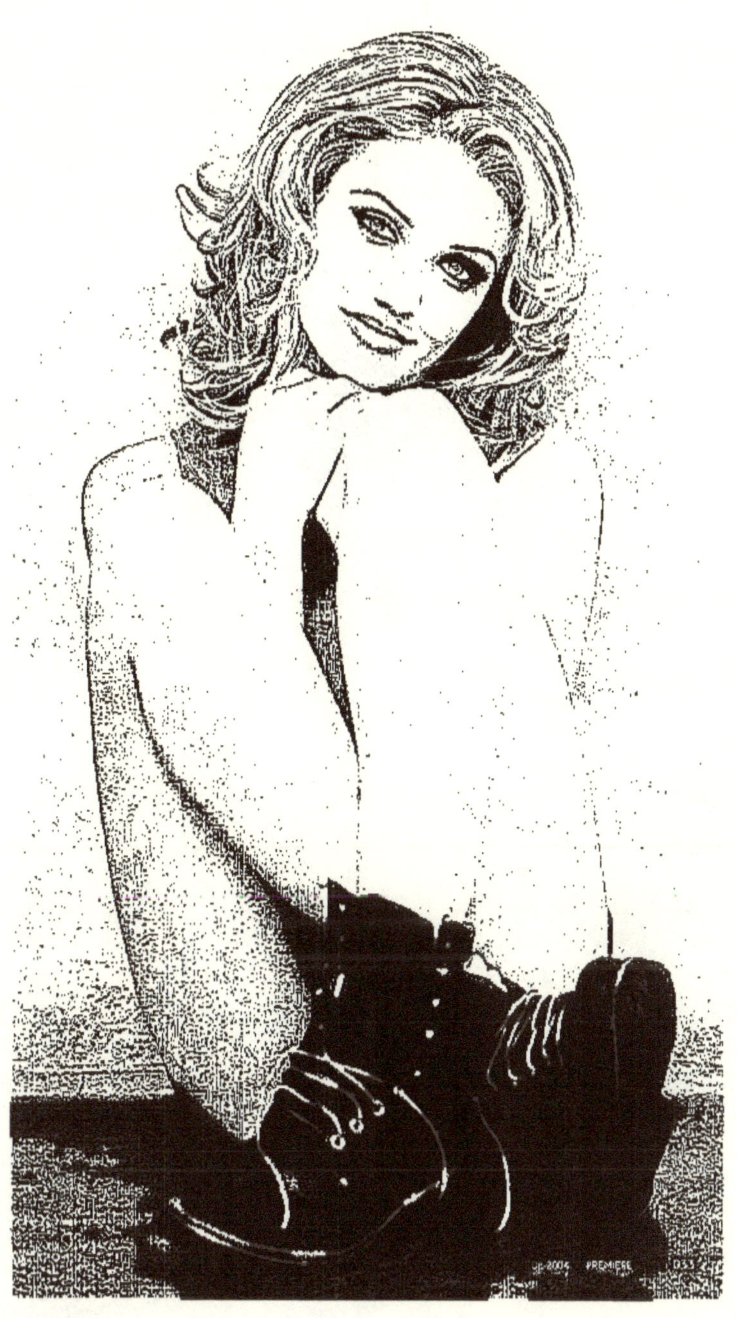
JB-2004 PREMIERE 033

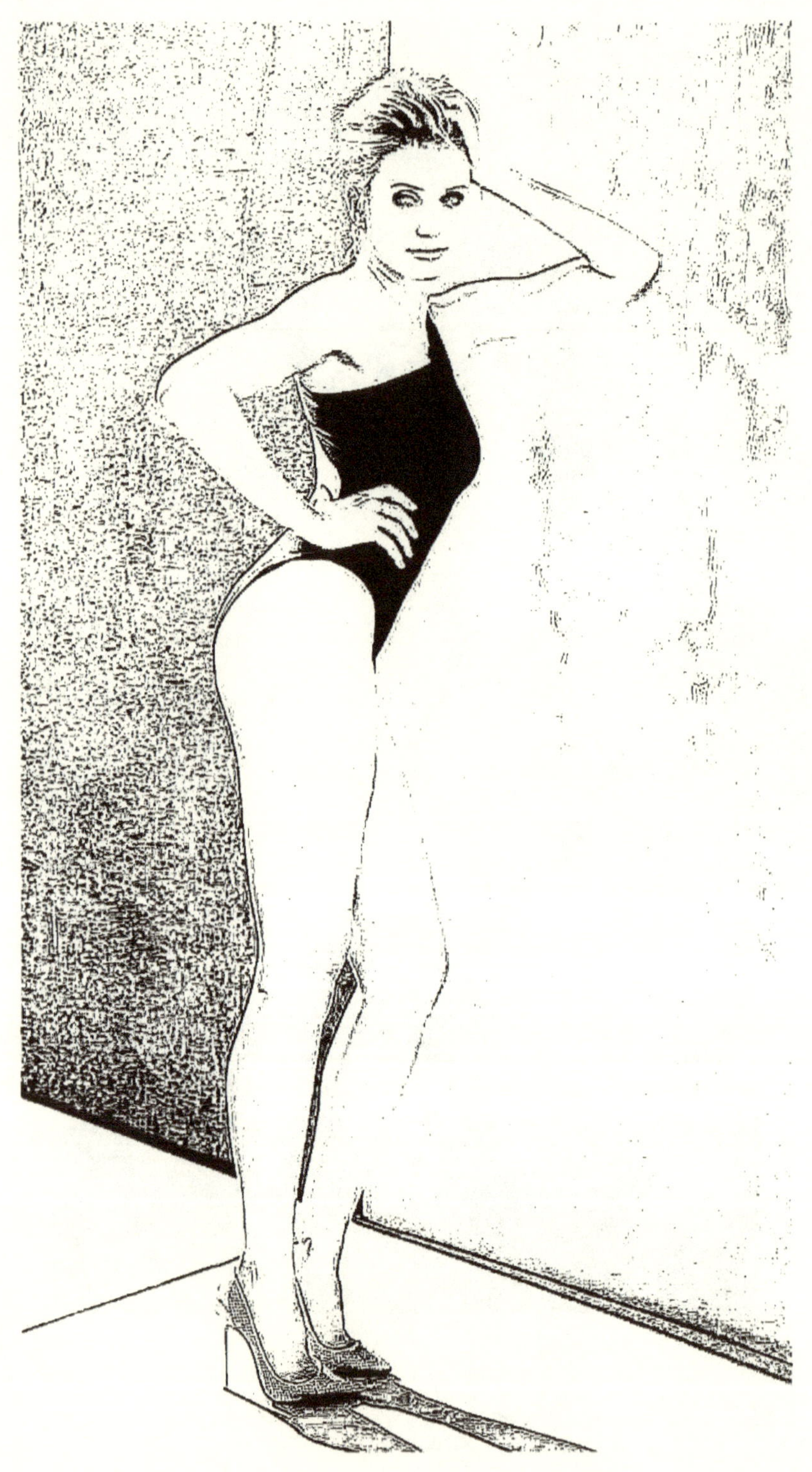

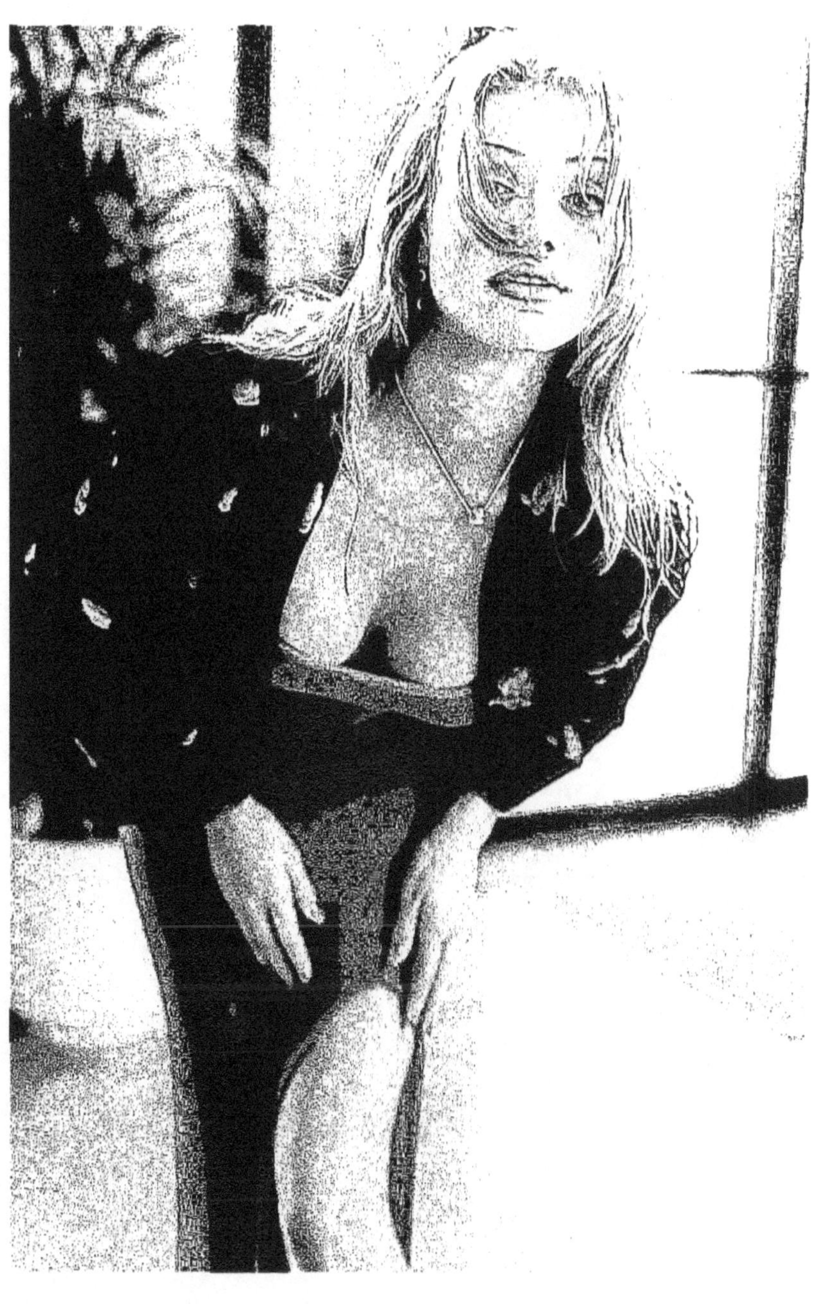

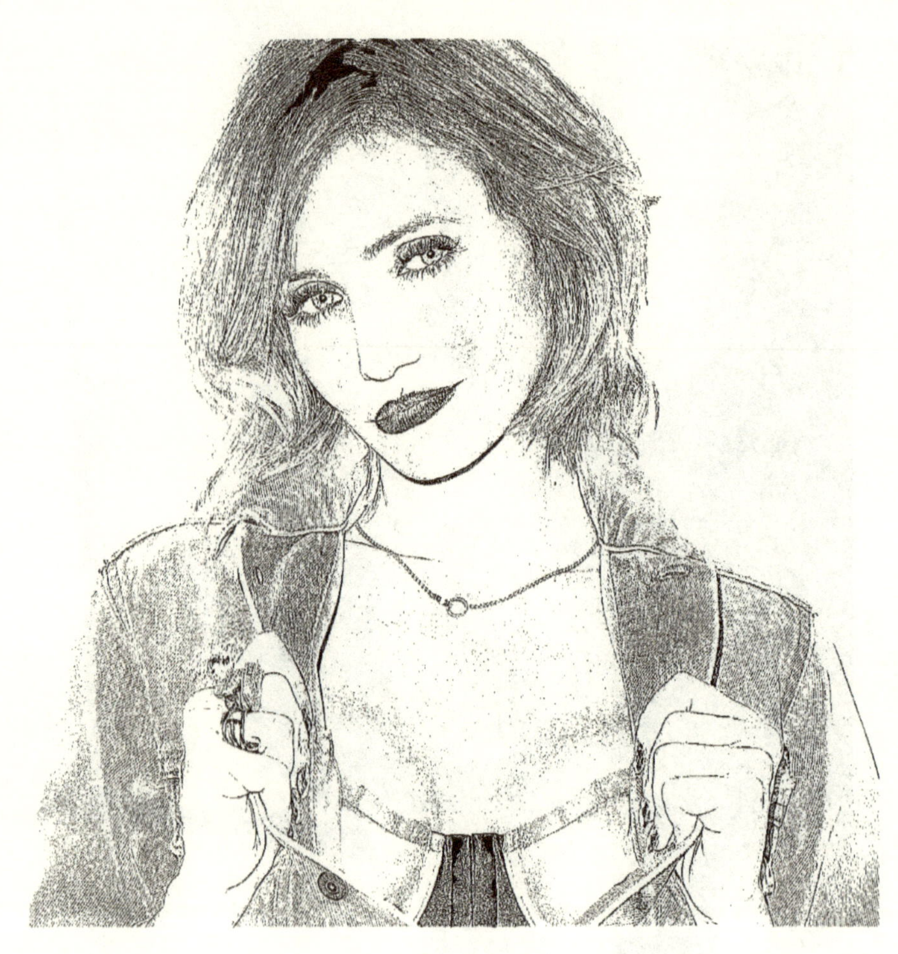

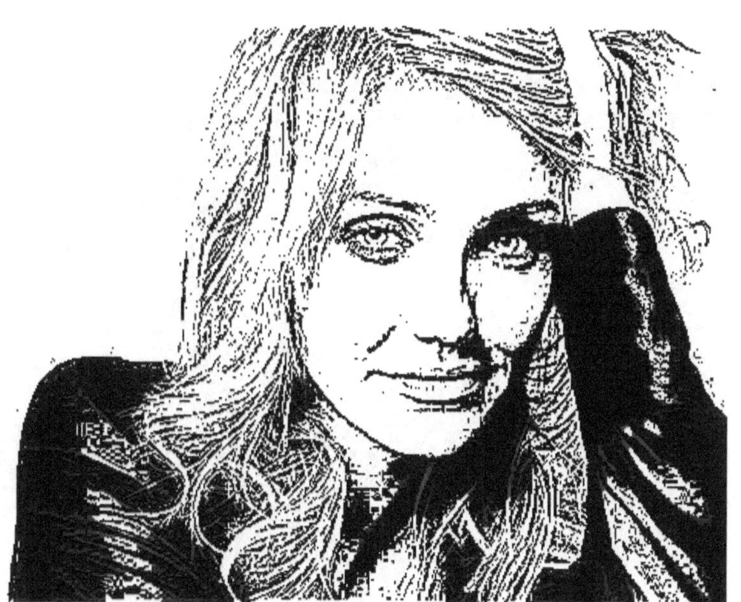

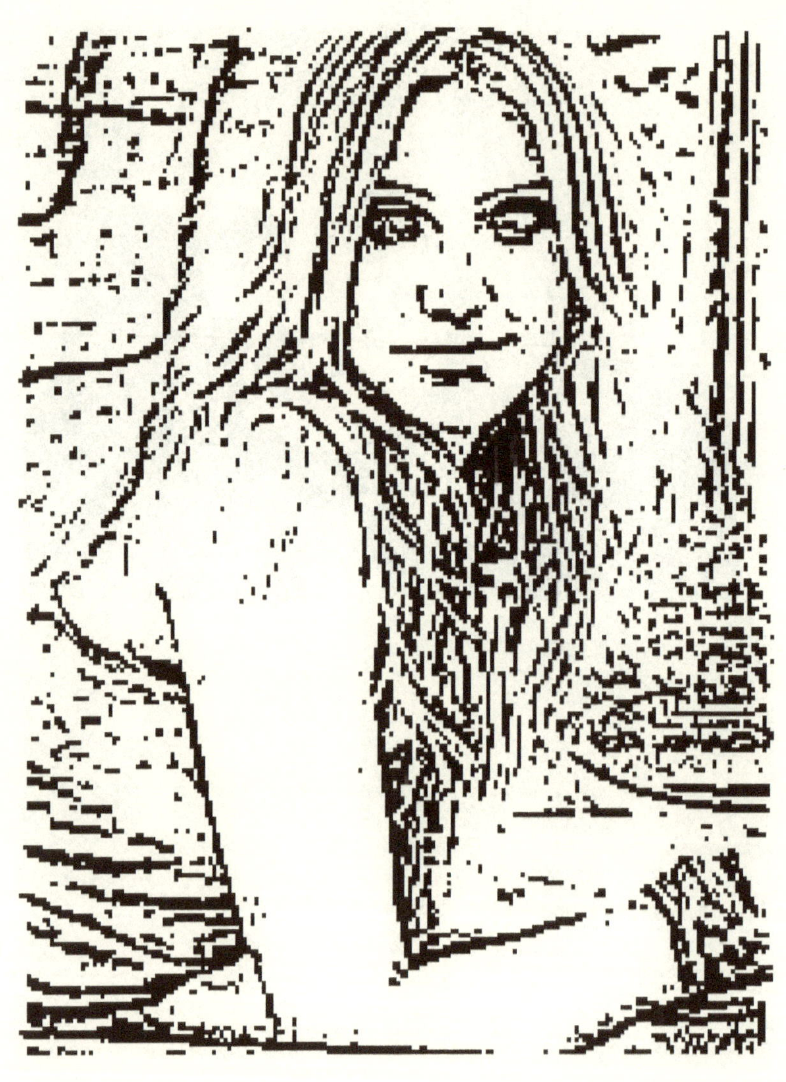

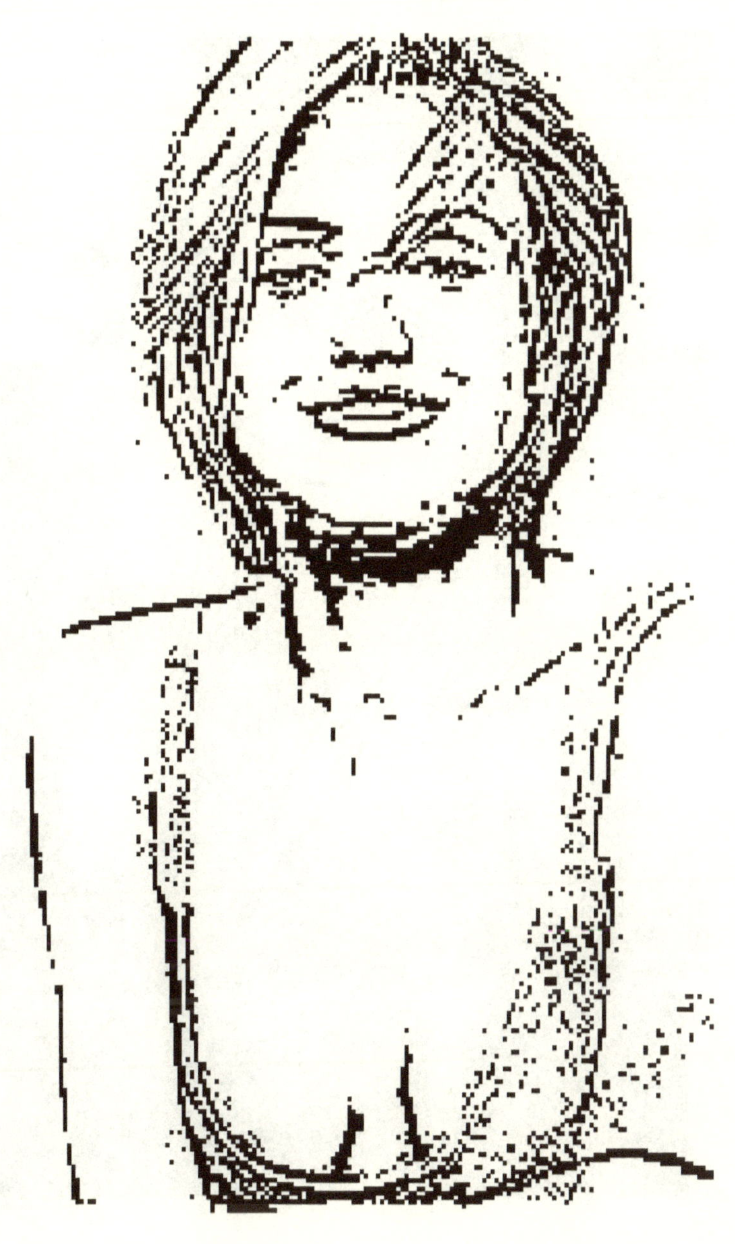

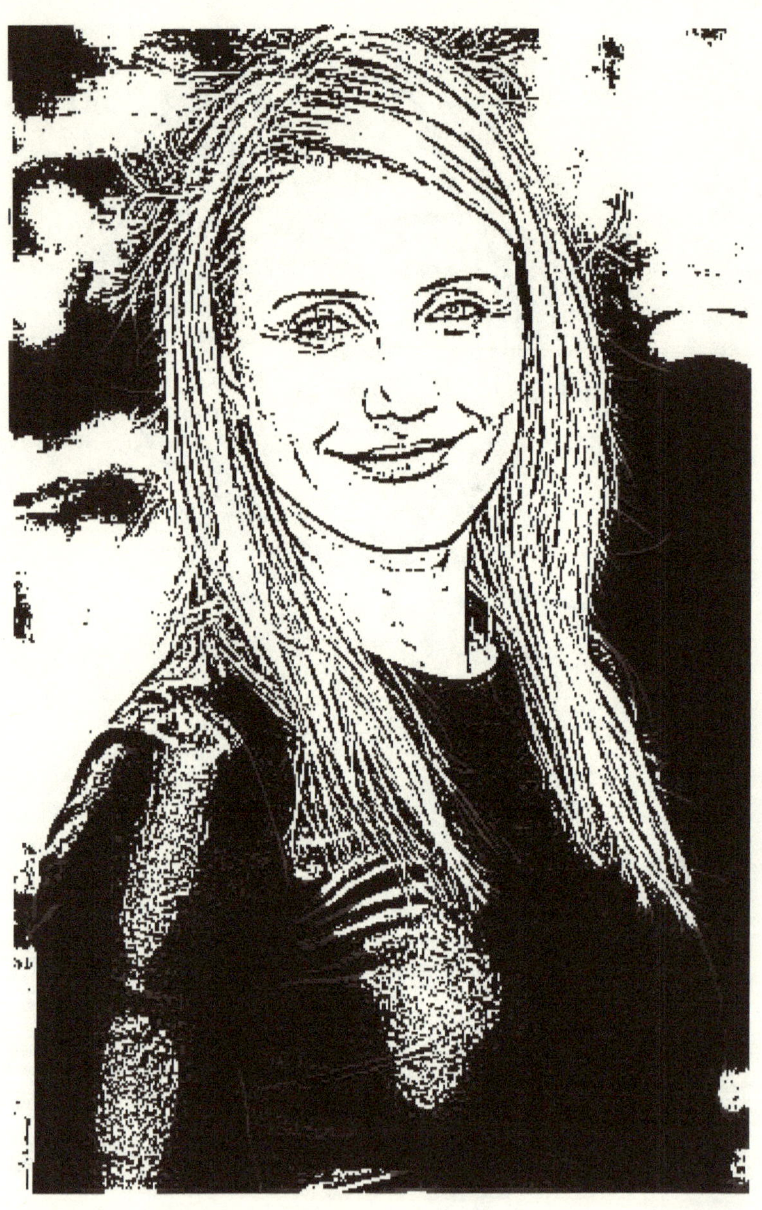

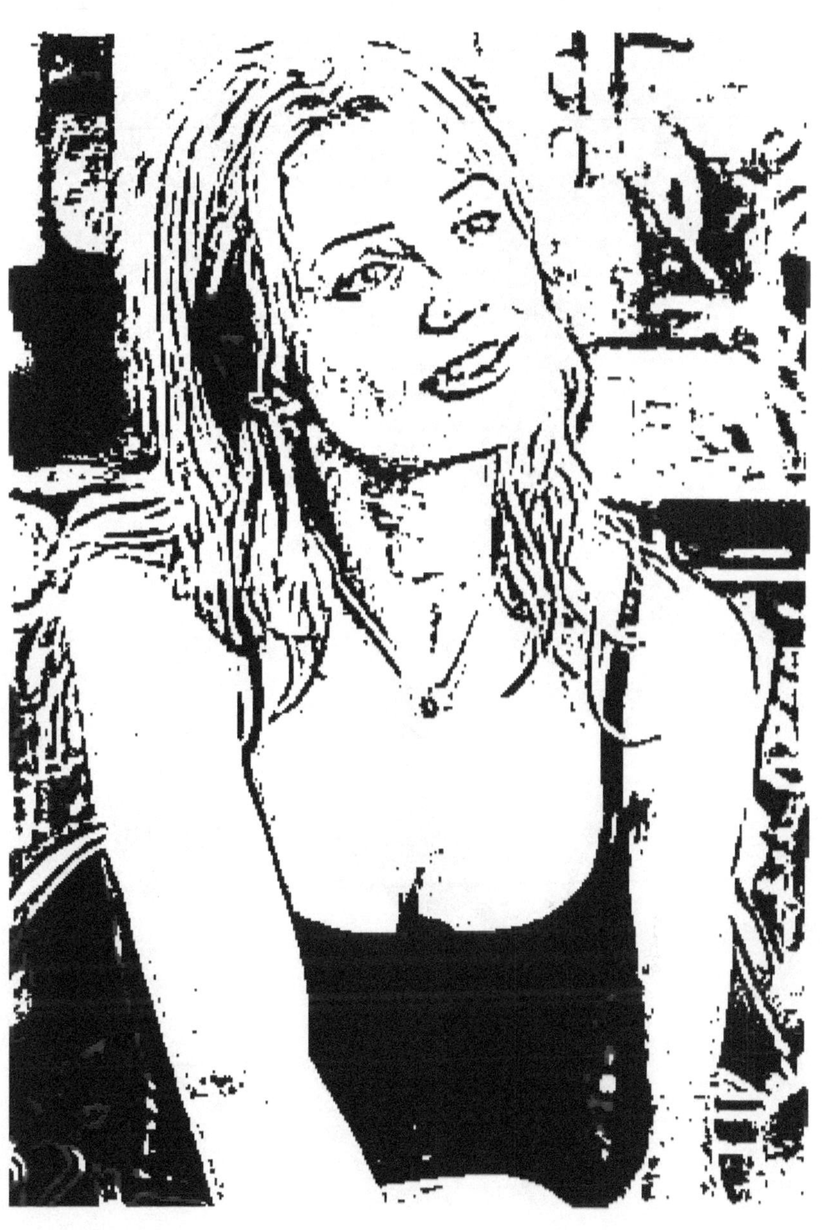

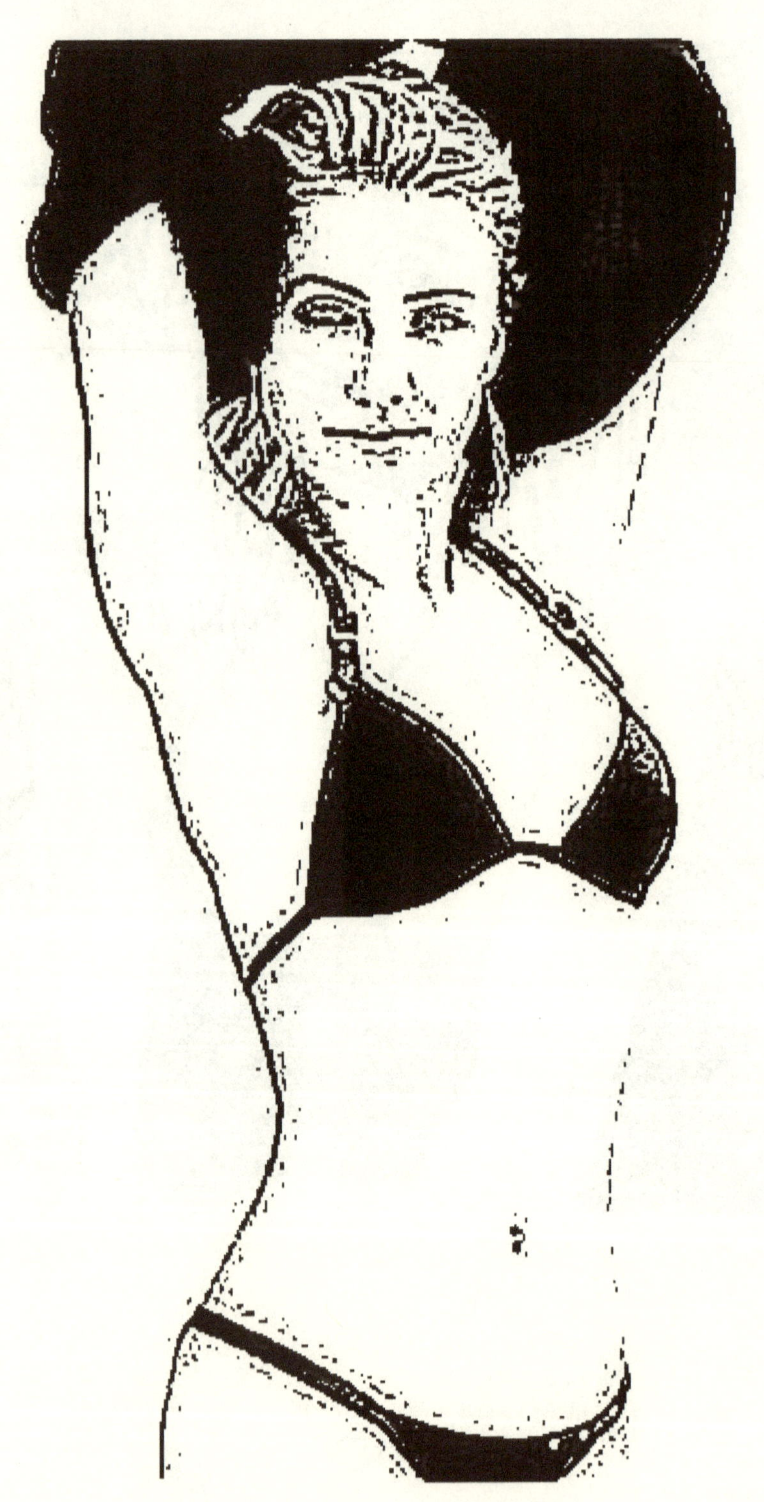